Soups
Classic to Contemporary

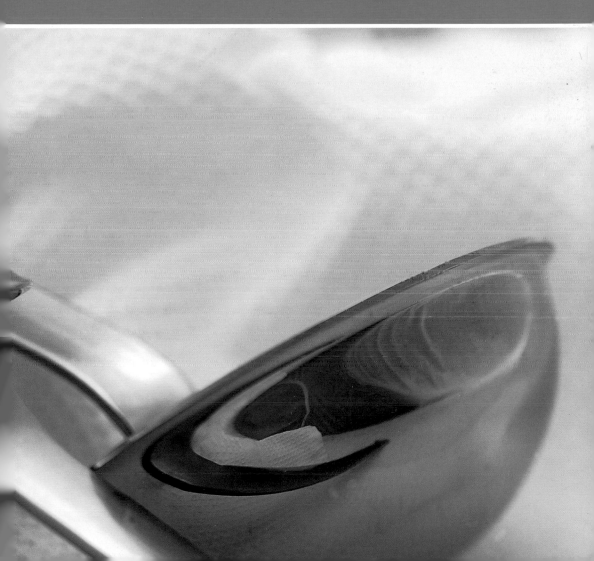

Contents

The ABC's of Soup

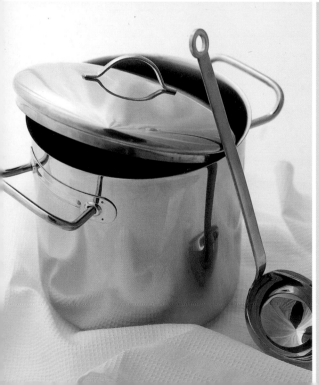

Recipes

Appendix

Soup Satisfies

There's nothing in the world like a bowl of really good soup— so invigorating, so warm and inviting, so comforting, and so practical because it is full of good things in a single pot. Soup is also so versatile that you can come up with a new creation every day. The trick to good soup is to start from scratch using these recipes instead of store-bought, five-minute soup mixes. In this book you'll find a little of everything, from regional classics to trendy newcomers. Read on and discover your next favorite!

Can Good Soup be Made in a Hurry?

Take Your Time

A really good soup is one of the finer things in life. It's too special to be made from store-bought mixes or re-heated from a can. Plus, there's no greater culinary achievement in the kitchen than transforming some liquid and a few humble ingredients into a mouth-watering soup—a hearty stock, a bunch of colorful vegetables, and a handful of green herbs become a fantastic pot of summer soup; asparagus broth, wine, and whipping cream become an elegant asparagus cream soup; or a few pieces of fresh salmon, seasonings such as

ginger and star anise, and a fragrant chicken stock become an exotic Asian soup bowl. Soups like these nourish you and the ones you love, body and soul.

Soup's on!

Soups are also well know for their ability to bring people together. From the young boy and his father sipping piping hot clam chowder from a thermos while fishing together to downtown diners packed side-by-side noisily slurping on steaming bowls at the counter of a bustling noodle bar in Shanghai, across the globe people enjoy sipping soup together. It's the age-old desire for nurturing comfort foods, and nothing satisfies quite like soup.

But, the best way to enjoy soup is right in your own home. That doesn't mean you'll have to be cooking all day long. This book takes away some of the mystery surrounding the making of soup. It gives you recipes for hearty meals made in

> **2** *The basis for many a favorite soup: good seasonings*

a single pot, for more refined creations suitable as first courses, and for flavorful clear broths and consommés finished with meats, vegetables, and noodles. These soups are guaranteed to make those who eat them swoon—at least for the duration of a meal.

> **1** *Anyone who loves chicken stock must have a big enough pot.*

The Classics

Soup can be divided into two basic categories — clear, thin soups and thick soups, which can be further subdivided into four more groups. The most important are described here.

Clear, Thin Soups

These soups are basically made up of water and flavoring. From fresh favorites such as asparagus broth to rich classics such as beef consommé, clear soups are based on a good stock started from bones, vegetables, or fish pieces. If meat or fish is added right at the start, then you have a consommé. A consommé can be simmered down to a rich, pure flavor or again supplemented with meat to make a double consommé.

Thick Soups

These include both traditional vegetable soups and any stews to which noodles, potatoes, rice, bread, etc. are added to make them a complete meal in a bowl.

Purée Soups

These soups are made by cooking vegetables in a liquid until tender. The mixture is then puréed or finely mashed which thickens and binds the soup. Otherwise they can be cooked with bread or potatoes as a thickener. Important: Fill the blender only halfway with warm soup; otherwise it will slosh over the sides.

Cream Soups

Typically a cream soup is made with equal parts of stock and heavy cream, which gives the soup body and a rich taste and texture. Wine, spices, or puréed vegetables give the soup its flavor profile. Cream soups taste best when blended until foamy.

Velouté Soups

Traditionally bound with flour: for 4 cups of soup, melt 2 tbs butter in a pan and brown 2 tbs flour until golden. Remove from heat and pour in hot liquid while stirring. Bring to a boil. Simmering for 10 minutes gets rid of the floury taste.

Bound Soups

Another technique used to make a cream soup is to use a "binder" of egg yolk and cream. To do so, stir together 4 egg yolks and 1 cup cream for 4 cups of soup. Remove hot soup from heat and stir a ladleful into the thickener. Then stir the thickener into the pot of soup. Heat soup without bringing to a boil.

Soup Bases

Global Player

A good homemade chicken stock cures many ills, above all any worries you might have about making a bad soup. That's why it's used as the base for some of the best soups in the world. In Asia and the Mediterranean, it is the most widely used stock. Even in Central Europe, it is slowly taking the place of beef stock in home cooking and veal stock in upscale cuisine. Here is an all-purpose recipe.

Chicken Stock

MAKES 12 CUPS:

- ➤ 1 stewing chicken (about 3⅓ lbs)
- 1 onion
- 1 clove garlic
- 2 each carrots, celery root, and parsnips
- 2 leeks
- 4 sprigs fresh thyme (or 1 tsp dried)
- 1 bay leaf
- ¼ lemon
- 10 peppercorns
- Salt

TIP

Keeps Well

Let freshly made chicken stock cool. It will keep 5 days in the refrigerator or 6 months in the freezer.

1 Submerge chicken in boiling water for 1 minute and then rinse under cold running water. Bring to a boil in 12 cups cold water, skimming foam often.

2 Peel onion and garlic and cut in half. Peel carrots, celery root, and parsnips and cut into pieces. Remove dark green parts from leeks and cut white parts in half lengthwise. Rinse well. Rinse herbs. Rinse and dry lemon under hot water, grate off zest, and squeeze out juice.

3 Simmer all ingredients, including pepper, with the chicken for 1 hour. Let chicken cool in the stock. Pour stock through a strainer, remove fat, bring to a boil, and season with salt.

On the Lighter Side

If you're making a vegetarian soup or a more delicate soup, you can use a vegetable stock —preferably homemade if it's flavorful enough. In this recipe we make sure it is by roasting the ingredients first, which also provides the stock with the necessary fat. The rest of the flavor is derived from herbs, spices, and soy sauce.

Vegetable Stock

MAKES 8 CUPS:

- ➤ 2 onions
  1 clove garlic
  3 each carrots, celery root, and parsnips
  3 leeks
  1 tomato
  1 bunch parsley
  3 1/2 oz mushrooms
  2 tbs olive oil
  10 peppercorns
  1 bay leaf
  2 tbs soy sauce | Salt

Fresh and Fast

You can keep cooled vegetable stock for 1 week in the refrigerator or 6 months in the freezer.

1 Peel onions and garlic and dice onions coarsely. Peel carrots, celery root, and parsnips, and dice about 1/2-inch thick. Cut dark green parts from leek and cut white parts in half lengthwise. Rinse well. Rinse tomato, core, and cut into quarters. Rinse parsley and wipe off mushrooms with a cloth.

2 Gently braise onions in oil for 10 minutes. Add and sauté root vegetables and leek over higher heat for 3–4 minutes until everything is slightly brown.

3 Bring vegetables to a boil in 10 cups hot water. Add all the other ingredients and gently simmer for 1 hour, then let stand 30 minutes. Pour through a strainer, bring to a boil, and season with salt.

7

From Crêpes to Crostini

Noodles

Makes approx. 10½ oz: Knead together 1½ cups plus 1 tbs flour, 2 eggs, ½ tsp salt, and ½ tsp oil to make a smooth dough. Brush dough with oil, wrap in a cloth, and set aside for 30 minutes. Then knead dough on a floured work surface and roll out into a very thin layer. Sprinkle with flour, roll it up, and cut it into thin noodles. Let noodles dry for 1–2 hours.

Cook noodles in salted water for 1–3 minutes (depending on how dry they are) until al dente and serve in clear soup.

Cheese Crostini

Toast 4 slices sandwich bread. Mix 5 oz grated cheese with 1 egg and 1 tbs oil and spread this mixture on the toast. Cut toast into quarters diagonally and cook under a hot broiler until they start to change color. Serve in cups of broth or consommé, or along side cream soups.

Crêpes

Stir together 2 eggs, 2 pinches salt, and 5 tbs flour, then mix with 5 tbs milk and 1 tbs chopped parsley until smooth. Season with pepper and let stand for 15 minutes. Brush a little oil onto a small frying pan, heat, and fry batter to make thin, golden pancakes.

Roll up warm pancakes and let cool. Then use a knife to cut them into thin strips and serve in broth or consommé.

Semolina Quenelle

Beat 2 tbs softened butter until creamy, then stir in 1 egg and finally ⅔ cup durum wheat semolina. Season with salt, pepper, and nutmeg and let stand for 10 minutes. Using wet teaspoons, make this mixture into oval balls. Place balls on a greased baking sheet and refrigerate for 20 minutes.

Then cook balls in gently simmering, salted water for 10 minutes. Serve in clear broth or consommé with chopped chives.

Meatballs

Dice 1 slice sandwich bread and mix with 2 tbs milk. Knead with 9 oz ground pork or ground beef and 1 egg yolk and season with salt and pepper. Moisten your hands, shape this mixture into hazelnut-sized balls, and refrigerate for 30 minutes. Then cook meatballs in gently simmering, salted water for 10 minutes. Remove from water with a slotted spoon and serve in clear soup or stews.

Herbed Toasts

Take 2 rolls that are not quite stale and cut crosswise into 1/3-inch slices. Whisk together 1 egg, 1/2 cup milk, 1 tbs chopped herbs, salt, and pepper. Dredge bread slices in the egg mixture. Melt 2 tbs butter in two pans and fry slices until golden. Let cool, cut slices crosswise into strips, and serve in broth or consommé or cream soup.

Dumplings

Stir together 3 eggs and 2/3 cup flour to make a smooth, runny mixture and season to taste with salt, pepper, and nutmeg. Using a wet teaspoon and your moistened fingertip, scrape spoonfuls of batter directly into boiling stock. Cook gently for 1–2 minutes and serve. Delicious in seasoned stocks and vegetable soups.

Crispy Bites

Instead of as a soup garnish, serve as a side dish with clear and creamy soups. Drain 1/3 cup sour cream. Cut 5 1/2 tbs cold butter into small pieces and, using your fingertips, blend together quickly with 2/3 cup flour and 1 pinch salt until crumbly. Add sour cream and blend until the dough holds together. Shape dough into a ball, wrap in plastic wrap, and refrigerate for 2 hours.

Then preheat oven to 350°F. On a floured work surface, roll out dough into a thin sheet and cut into 3/4-inch-wide strips and the length of a finger. Brush with 1 whisked egg yolk and bake in the oven for 20 minutes.

Soup for Company

When guest are coming over, think soup. It can serve as an invigorating hors d'oeuvre, an elegant first course, or a casual one-bowl supper. Best of all, it can satisfy the hunger of large numbers of people without you having to be tied to the kitchen. Start out by making the right amount: 2 cups per person is enough for a meal, 1 cup per person as part of a full-course dinner or buffet, including a second helping. As an hors d'oeuvre, ¾ cup will do.

The Perfect Finish

Soup is also the ideal party food because you can prepare it ahead of time. Whether a

1 The perfect meal for company: Soup is easy to prepare ahead of time.

clear broth or a delicate purée soup, often all you need to do is heat it up and add a few finishing touches before serving. But keep the following in mind:

➤ Thick soups may separate slightly when reheated so prepare just before serving.

➤ A cream soup tastes best if you wait to add the cream until the very end.

➤ Although stews often taste better after reheating, you won't have crispy vegetables or al dente noodles unless you add them within an hour of serving.

➤ Soup will stay warm longer in pre-warmed bowls or cups. To achieve a rustic, old-world style, ladle the soup from a tureen on the table. Or for something different, serve hearty soups in coffee mugs or delicate soups in tea cups.

2 Not enough bowls in your cupboard? Soup also tastes great in coffee mugs.

➤ Once the soup is ready, get it to the table immediately. Otherwise soup garnishes will start to look like they've passed their prime.

Serving Tip

When serving up a ladle of soup, briefly dip the base of the ladle back into the soup to keep from dripping when you transfer it to a bowl.

What can I do if...

...the soup is too thin?

> In this case, use a butter-flour mixture as a thickener: using your fingertips, quickly blend together 1 part softened butter and 1 part flour, whisk it into the hot soup, and briefly bring to a boil. Make sure you simmer long enough to cook off any floury taste.

...the soup is too thick?

> Remove a little soup and add hot stock a little at a time until the appropriate consistency is achieved. Make sure the stock you add is hot, which will give you a true consistency immediately.

...the soup is too heavily seasoned?

> A pinch of sugar will tone down a salty or acidic taste, or else a healthy dash of cream or water. But be careful not to kill all the flavor by watering it down. It's better to start out conservatively. So for stocks that are cooked for a long time, don't add salt until the very end.

...the soup tastes really bland?

> Season it, of course. But you don't have to use salt alone. You can often intensify the flavor with a little lemon, a pinch sugar, or some fresh herbs. But keep in mind that some spices and firmer herbs need a little time for the their flavor to unfold whereas tender herbs quickly lose their aroma.

...the stock came out cloudy?

> Remedy: Whisk together 1 egg white and 1 dash lemon juice, then stir into 8 cups cold stock and heat until the foam starts to solidify.
>
> Simmer for 15 minutes without stirring and let stand for 15 minutes. Skim off foam and pour soup through a cheese cloth.

...the soup separated?

> This can be caused by the reaction of dairy products or egg to too much acid or by too much boiling. In this case, prepare a roux (see velouté soups, page 5), add it to a little cooled soup while stirring, simmer gently for 10 minutes, and blend together vigorously.

...I burned the soup?

> First of all, get it out of the pot. If it's only slightly burnt, you can cover the taste with cream, stock, something acidic, something sweet, or spices. But if the whole thing tastes bad, you'll have to throw it away and start over.

...the soup looks boring?

> A dollop of crème fraîche or whipped cream dresses up a puréed soup. Herb butter is also a possibility, even on a stew. Pesto or drizzled olive oil give it a Mediterranean flair, as does mayonnaise flavored with garlic or lemon.

...I have soup left over?

> No problem! You can eat soup anywhere, anytime, and it tastes even better the second time around!

11

Colorful Stockpots

A small, elegant soup makes a lovely beginning to a multi-course dinner party, but real soup fans would prefer to have soup as the meal's main star. Here you'll find heartwarming soups full of nutritious vegetables and other good things, perfect for lunch or a light dinner accompanied by a salad and some crusty bread.

Quick Recipes

Fast Asian Hot Pot

SERVES 4:

➤ 7 oz shiitake mushrooms
  1 bunch radishes with greens (14 oz)
  5 oz sugar peas | 2 smoked chicken
  thighs (refrigerated section of market;
  may substitute ¹/₂ roasted chicken)
  4 cups chicken stock | 3 tbs soy sauce
  2 tbs Chinese rice wine (may substitute
  sherry or stock)

1 | Clean mushrooms and slice thinly. Clean
radishes, rinse, pull off leaves, and slice bulbs
thinly. Clean sugar peas, rinse, and cut into
fine strips. Mix together all these ingredients. Peel skin from chicken, remove meat
from the bones, and shred or dice.

2 | Bring remaining ingredients to a boil.
Set aside 4 tbs vegetables and bring the
rest to a boil in the soup. Remove soup
from heat, add chicken, and let stand for
3 minutes. Transfer soup to bowls and
sprinkle raw vegetables over the top.

Spring Onion Soup

SERVES 4:

➤ 8 green onions | ¹/₂ tsp sugar
  2 tbs butter | 1 cup hard cider
  4 cups fish stock | 1 bay leaf
  10 oz white fish filet
  Salt | Cayenne pepper
  3¹/₂ oz cooked, small bay shrimp

1 | Rinse green onions, clean, remove
dark green parts, and cut into rings.
Gently braise onions and sugar in
butter for 3 minutes. Pour in 5 tbs
hard cider and reduce. Add remaining
cider, stock, and bay leaf and simmer
gently for 5 minutes.

2 | Cut fish into very thin slices and
distribute in four soup bowls. Season
green onion soup with salt and cayenne.
Heat shrimp in the soup and pour hot
soup over the fish. Serve immediately.

13

Mediterranean | Vegetarian
Summer Soup with Aioli

SERVES 4–6:
- 1 small cauliflower
- 14 oz green beans
- 20 cherry tomatoes (9 oz)
- 3 cloves garlic
- 1 tsp saffron
- 4 sprigs fresh thyme (may substitute ½ tsp dried)
- Salt
- 1 bay leaf
- 1 bunch basil
- Pepper
- ½ cup mayonnaise

⏲ Prep time: 45 minutes
- Calories per serving: 185

1 | Clean cauliflower, cut into bite-size florets, and rinse. Rinse beans, clean, and cut into 1-inch pieces. Rinse cherry tomatoes and cut into quarters. Peel garlic. Soak saffron in 5 tbs warm water. Rinse thyme, shake dry, and pull off leaves.

2 | Bring to a boil 6 cups water, ½ tsp salt, garlic, bay leaf, and thyme. Cook beans for 3 minutes, then add cauliflower and cook another 8–10 minutes until the vegetables are al dente. In the meantime, rinse basil, shake dry, and chop leaves coarsely.

3 | Remove bay leaf and garlic from the soup. Discard bay leaf and set aside garlic. Add cherry tomatoes and saffron including the soaking liquid to the soup and briefly bring to a boil. Season soup with salt and pepper and remove from heat. Stir in basil, cover, and let stand for 5 minutes.

4 | In the meantime, mash garlic with a fork and mix with mayonnaise. Transfer soup to bowls and top each serving with a generous dollop of garlic mayonnaise.

TIP

Homemade Aioli

Translating "aioli" as "garlic mayonnaise" is like calling pesto a basil sauce—too flat. In Provence, this sauce mixed with olive oil is an elixir of life much like that of a good cup of coffee in the morning. The people there use it for seasoning, spreading on bread, as a soup garnish, or as part of a main dish. Here's how to make it: Depending on your personal preference, peel 3–5 cloves garlic and squeeze through a press or, more authentically, chop coarsely and crush in a mortar with salt. Stir together garlic, 1 egg yolk, and a dash of lemon juice. Then, using a wire whisk or hand mixer, beat in $2/3$–1 cup extra virgin olive oil in a thin stream. Season to taste with salt, lemon, and a little cayenne pepper. (Yields about 1 cup aioli.)

Spicy | For Company

Red Stew with Parmesan Butter

SERVES 4:

- 6 tbs softened butter
- 2 oz freshly grated Parmesan
- 1/2 tsp lemon juice
- Salt and pepper
- 2 red onions
- 1/2 fresh red chill pepper (optional)
- 2 red bell peppers
- 1 tbs Hungarian sweet paprika
- 1 (14 1/2-oz) can peeled tomatoes
- 1/2 cup fruity red wine
- 1 pinch sugar

🕐 Prep time: 40 minutes
➤ Calories per serving: 305

1 | Using your fingertips, quickly blend together 3 tbs butter, Parmesan, and lemon juice and season with salt and pepper. Shape into a cylinder, wrap in plastic wrap, and refrigerate.

2 | Peel onions and dice. Clean chili pepper, remove seeds, and chop finely. Rinse bell peppers, clean, and dice.

3 | Braise onions and chili pepper in remaining butter, covered and over low heat, for 10 minutes. Add diced bell peppers and paprika and braise for another minute. Then add tomatoes including liquid, red wine, and 2 1/2 cups water and bring to a boil.

4 | Season stew with salt, pepper, and sugar and cook for 15–20 minutes until the diced bell pepper is tender. Mash ingredients coarsely, transfer to soup bowls, and garnish each with one slice of Parmesan butter.

Traditional
Heartwarming

White Stew with Leek Cream

SERVES 4:

- 1 large leek
- 2 kohlrabi
- 2 tbs butter
- 2 tbs flour
- 4 cups cold vegetable stock
- 1 cup milk
- Salt, pepper, and nutmeg
- 3/4 cup canned, cooked white beans
- 1/4 cup crème fraîche

🕐 Prep time: 40 minutes
➤ Calories per serving: 305

1 | Clean leek, cut in half lengthwise, and rinse. Cut light green and white parts into strips and set both aside while keeping separate. Peel kohlrabi, cut into wedges, and slice wedges thinly.

2 | Braise white parts of leek in butter, covered, over low heat, for 3 minutes. Add kohlrabi and braise for another minute, then sprinkle with flour and brown the flour. Set aside 5 tbs vegetable stock and add remaining stock and the milk to vegetables while stirring. Bring to a boil, season with salt, pepper, and nutmeg, add white beans, and cook for 15 minutes until the vegetables are tender.

3 | In the meantime, braise light green leeks with remaining vegetable stock, covered in a small pot, for 10 minutes until tender. Let cool, then mix in crème fraîche.

4 | Season stew to taste, transfer to soup bowls, and top each serving with a dollop of leek cream.

Traditional with a New Twist | Inexpensive

Fall Soup with Mustard Cream

SERVES 4–6:

➤ **1 onion**
¹/₂ head savoy cabbage (17 oz)
1 lb carrots
1 tbs dried marjoram
2 tbs oil
Salt
2 apples
1 tbs apple cider vinegar
1 cup sour cream
3 tbs mustard
1 lb pre-cooked bratwurst (or other mild sausage)

⏲ Prep time. 1 hour
➤ Calories per serving (6): 420

1 | Peel onion and dice finely. Cut half savoy cabbage in halves and cut out core and thick ribs on leaves. Cut leaves into squares and then rinse in a colander. Peel carrots, quarter lengthwise, and cut into 2-inch slices.

2 | Braise onions and marjoram in oil over low heat for 5 minutes. Add wet cabbage and carrots and braise another 2 minutes. Pour in 8 cups water, season with salt, and cook vegetables for 15–20 minutes until al dente.

3 | In the meantime, cut apples with the peels into quarters, remove cores, slice thinly, and mix with vinegar. Stir together sour cream and mustard and place on the table.

4 | Add apples and vinegar to soup and briefly bring to a boil, then add bratwurst. Cover, remove from heat, and let stand for 15 minutes. Remove sausage and peel, then cut into 4–6 pieces, and distribute in bowls. Season soup with salt and pepper to taste and transfer to bowls while hot. Garnish at the table with a dollop of mustard cream.

Cut savoy cabbage

Cut the half-head into two quarters.

2 **Remove core**

Cut out core and thick ribs on leaves.

3 **Cut into strips**

Cut quarters lengthwise into strips.

4 **Cut up and clean**

Cut strips crosswise into squares and rinse in a colander.

Easy | Heartwarming

Smoky Bacon and Carrot Soup

SERVES 4–6:

➤ 1 bunch parsley
1/2 lemon
1 bay leaf
1 tbs sugar
1 piece cinnamon stick (3/4 inch)
14 oz bacon
1 1/2 oz carrots
3 tbs butter
3 tbs flour
Salt

🕑 Prep time: 1 hour
➤ Calories per serving (6): 500

1 | Rinse parsley, shake dry, chop leaves finely, and set aside stems. Rinse lemon under hot water and dry, grate off zest from half, and squeeze out juice.

2 | Bring 4 1/2 cups water to a boil with parsley stems, lemon zest, bay leaf, sugar, and cinnamon and gently simmer bacon for 20 minutes. Remove bacon and pour water through a fine strainer. Set aside bacon and water.

3 | Peel carrots, dice, and sauté gently in butter for 5 minutes. Sprinkle with flour and brown for 1 minute while stirring. Add reserved water to carrots and cook for 10–15 minutes until al dente.

4 | Dice bacon. Stir into finished soup along with parsley and lemon juice. Reheat without bringing to a boil. For a heartier dish, serve with dumplings added to the soup.

Scottish
For Special Occasions

Hearty Winter Soup

SERVES 4–6:

➤ 4 leeks (1 3/4 lbs)
1 3/4 lbs beef stew meat
1 stewing chicken, rinsed and dried (3 lbs)
Salt and pepper

🕑 Prep time: 30 minutes
🕑 Cooking time: 3 hours
➤ Calories per serving (6): 350

1 | Remove dark green parts of leeks and discard. Cut half the leeks in half lengthwise, rinse well, and tie into a bundle using kitchen string. Cut remaining leeks into rings, rinse thoroughly, and set aside.

2 | Slowly bring stew meat to a boil along with bundled leeks in 12 cups cold water. Skim off foam and simmer meat gently for 2 1/2 hours until firm.

3 | After cooking for 2 1/2 hours, remove leek bundle and add chicken. If necessary, add water. Simmer soup for another 45 minutes, then remove from heat and let stand for 20 minutes, or until chicken is cooked through.

4 | Take beef and chicken out of the soup, remove skin from chicken, and cut into bite-size pieces. Season soup with salt and pepper. Add and simmer leek rings for 1 minute until al dente, then add meat back in and gently heat. Serve in large bowls.

Loaded Spoons

Now let's get down to the nitty-gritty. It's time to load up your spoon with all the things that make a soup hearty and satisfying: noodles and rice, lentils and beans, potatoes and bread. And when you also consider all the fresh garden herbs, fragrant spices, and invigorating essences, there's no excuse for serving a boring soup ever again!

Quick Recipes

Moroccan Breakfast Soup

SERVES 4:

- ➤ 1 clove garlic | 1 chili pepper
  1 bunch parsley | 2 tsp ground cumin
  Salt | 4 cups chicken stock
  1 (14 1/2-oz) can garbanzo beans
  2 pieces flatbread (3 1/2 oz)
  2 tbs capers | 4 very fresh eggs

1 | Peel garlic. Clean chili pepper and remove seeds. Chop both ingredients. Rinse parsley and pull off leaves. Bring stock to a boil with garlic, chili pepper, cumin, and a pinch of salt. Drain garbanzo beans, add, and simmer for 10 minutes.

2 | Slice bread and toast under the broiler or in an ungreased pan. Cut into smaller pieces, distribute in soup bowls along with parsley and capers, break an egg over each, and pour hot soup over the top.

Polenta Soup with Prosciutto

SERVES 4:

- ➤ 4 slices prosciutto | 2 tbs butter
  1 clove garlic | 1/3 cup cornmeal
  6 cups chicken stock | Salt and pepper
  1 slice toasted sandwich bread
  2 1/2 oz freshly grated Parmesan
  2 very fresh eggs

1 | Cut prosciutto into 1/3-inch-wide strips . Then, in a pot, brown in butter and remove. Peel garlic, dice, and sauté in pan drippings until translucent. Add and sauté cornmeal for 1 minute. Stir in all but 5 tbs of the stock, season with salt and pepper, and simmer for 10 minutes.

2 | Crumble toast between your hands and combine with 1 1/2 oz Parmesan, eggs, and remaining stock. Using a wire whisk, stir into gently simmering soup. Bring to a boil. Transfer to bowls and garnish with prosciutto and remaining Parmesan.

23

Exotic | Heartwarming

Asian Chicken Noodle Soup

SERVES 4:

➤ 1 stewing chicken (3 lbs)

3 cloves garlic

1 piece fresh ginger (walnut-sized)

6 green onions

1 cup soy sauce

1 cup rice wine (may substitute medium dry sherry)

1 cinnamon stick (2 inches)

1/3 cup sugar

4 eggs

9 oz Chinese wheat noodles (may substitute linguine)

Salt

🕐 Prep time: 1 hour

🕐 Cooling time: 2 hours

➤ Calories per serving: 650

1 | Rinse chicken inside and out under cold water and pat dry. Peel garlic and ginger and slice thinly. Rinse and clean green onions. Cut up dark green parts, cut lighter parts on an angle into fine rings, cover, and refrigerate.

2 | Find a pot just big enough to hold the chicken and bring 6 cups water to a boil with soy sauce, rice wine, ginger, cinnamon, garlic, onion greens, and sugar. Simmer gently for 20 minutes. Then insert the chicken with the breast side up and simmer for 20 minutes more. Turn chicken and simmer for another 5 minutes. Then cover the pot, remove from heat, and let cool for 2 hours. In the meantime, gently boil eggs for 8 minutes.

3 | Cut apart cooled chicken, remove skin, remove meat from bones, and dice. Pour stock through a fine strainer. Cook noodles in salted water according to the directions on the package, drain, and rinse under cold water. Peel eggs and slice.

4 | Bring stock back to a boil, then add noodles and chicken and heat without boiling. Transfer soup to large bowls and garnish at the table with onion rings and egg slices.

TIP

Gently Simmer Chicken

This traditional Asian noodle soup will give you the strength to face your toughest day. It's important that the chicken only simmer gently and that it not be completely done cooking until it has cooled. It's also important that you not boil the meat when you heat it for the last time as this will make it tough.

Mediterranean
For Company

Bean Soup

SERVES 4:

➤ ³⁄₄ cup dried white beans

2 cloves garlic

6 anchovies

¹⁄₄ cup dried tomatoes in oil

1 bay leaf

Salt and pepper

1 cup short macaroni

¹⁄₄ cup pesto

🕐 Prep time: 30 minutes

🕐 Soaking time: 12 hours

🕐 Cooking time: 1¹⁄₂ hours

➤ Calories per serving: 380

1 | Soak beans in cold water for 12 hours. Peel and dice garlic. Rinse anchovies under cold water and chop. Drain tomatoes and cut into strips, setting aside oil.

2 | In a pot, heat 4 tbs tomato oil and braise garlic and anchovies over low heat for 3 minutes. Add 6 cups water. Drain beans. Add beans and bay leaf to garlic-anchovy water and cook for 1¹⁄₄ to 1¹⁄₂ hours until al dente.

3 | Season bean soup with salt and pepper and add a little water if necessary. Bring to a boil. Add macaroni and cook for 8–10 minutes until al dente. Stir in tomatoes. Remove soup from heat, let stand for 3 minutes, and serve with 1 dollop of pesto in each bowl.

Inexpensive
Heartwarming

Barley Soup with Pork Meatballs

SERVES 4:

➤ 2 leeks

¹⁄₂ tsp caraway seeds

4 tbs clarified butter

No more than 8 cups beef or vegetable stock

1 cup pearl barley

1 slice sandwich bread

9 oz ground pork

1 egg yolk

2 tbs chopped parsley

Salt and pepper

🕐 Prep time: 35 minutes

🕐 Cooling time: 40 minutes

➤ Calories per serving: 605

1 | For the soup: Clean leeks, removing dark green parts. Cut in half lengthwise, rinse well, and cut crosswise into strips. Set aside light green strips. In 1 tbs clarified butter, braise white leek strips and caraway seeds for 1 minute. Pour in 7 cups stock and cook barley for 30–40 minutes until soft. If necessary, add more stock.

2 | For the meatballs: Chop bread and mix with ground pork, egg yolk, parsley, and 5 tbs stock. Season with salt and pepper, and with moistened hands, shape into ³⁄₄-inch balls. In a pan, heat remaining clarified butter, fry meatballs on all sides for 5 minutes, and remove from pan. Then fry light green leek strips for 3 minutes.

3 | Season barley soup to taste with salt and pepper. Stir in meatballs and leeks, remove from heat, and let stand for 5 minutes.

Middle-Eastern
Traditional

Lentils and Lamb

SERVES 4:

➤ 14 oz lamb (leg)
1 onion
2 yellow bell peppers
8 tbs olive oil
2 tbs garam masala
(Indian spice mixture; may
substitute curry powder)
1 (14½-oz) can
diced tomatoes
¾ cup red lentils
1 bunch mint
1 lemon
¼ cup bulgur
Salt and pepper

⏱ Prep time: 1 hour
➤ Calories per serving: 505

1 | Cut lamb into 1 inch cubes. Peel and dice onion. Rinse bell peppers, clean, remove seeds, and dice.

2 | Place oil and onions in a pan, cover, and braise over low heat for 10 minutes. Add meat and bell peppers and sauté over high heat for 2–3 minutes, then add garam masala and cook briefly. Pour in tomatoes and 4 cups water.

Add lentils and cook for 15–20 minutes until tender.

3 | Rinse mint and chop leaves. Squeeze juice from lemon. Combine juice, mint, and bulgur, let stand for 15 minutes and then stir into lentil stew. Bring to a boil, season with salt and pepper, remove from heat, and let stand for 5 minutes.

For Company

Lentil Orange Soup

SERVES 4:

➤ 1¼ cup brown lentils
8 oranges
1 clove garlic
½ tsp fennel seeds
4 tbs olive oil
¾ cup dry white wine
2¼ cup fish stock
1 bay leaf
1 bunch basil
10½ oz white fish filet
Salt and pepper

⏱ Prep time: 40 minutes
⏱ Soaking time: 4 hours
⏱ Cooking time: 40 minutes
➤ Calories per serving: 700

1 | Rinse lentils in a colander, pick over, and dry. Set aside 2 oranges and squeeze juice out of the rest until you have 2 cups juice. Soak lentils in this juice for 4 hours.

2 | Rinse remaining 2 oranges under hot water, dry, and grate off zest. Then peel completely, removing white membrane. With a pointy knife, remove segments from white skins, saving the juice. Squeeze juice from the orange scraps.

3 | Peel garlic and dice. Sauté garlic and fennel seeds in 1 tbs oil, then pour in wine. Add lentils with the juice, stock, 1 cup water, orange zest, and bay leaf and simmer for 30–40 minutes until al dente. Rinse basil, shake dry, and chop leaves coarsely.

4 | Cut fish into strips 1¼ inch wide and season with salt and pepper. Sauté strips in remaining oil for 1 minute on each side and place in soup bowls. Stir basil, orange segments, and remaining juice into soup, season with salt and pepper, and pour over fish.

Heartwarming | Easy

Old-Fashioned Potato Soup

SERVES 4–6:

➤ 2 each carrots, celery root, and parsnips

2 leeks

9 oz bacon

2¼ lbs waxy potatoes

1 tbs oil

½ tsp caraway seeds

1 tsp dried marjoram

6 cups beef or vegetable stock

Salt

Pepper

Nutmeg

7 tbs herb butter

🕐 Prep time: 50 minutes

➤ Calories per serving (6): 500

1 | Peel carrots, celery root, and parsnips and cut into ⅓-inch cubes. Cut dark green parts from leek, then slice down middle lengthwise and rinse well. Cut leek into ⅓-inch pieces. Remove rind from bacon and dice bacon finely. Rinse potatoes, peel, and dice to same size as carrots, celery root, and parsnips.

2 | In a large pot, fry bacon in oil until crispy, remove, and set aside. Braise leeks, carrots, celery root, parsnips, caraway seeds, and marjoram in bacon fat for 5 minutes, then add stock, potatoes, and bacon rind and cook for 15–20 minutes until almost tender.

3 | Remove bacon rind. Pour half the soup into another pot and mash with a potato masher. Return mashed soup to the first pot and season with salt, pepper, and nutmeg.

4 | Cut herb butter into 4–6 portions. Heat up soup and transfer to soup bowls. Add one piece butter to each bowl and serve this old-fashioned potato soup immediately.

TIP

Potato Soup à la Savoyarde

Leave it to the French to come up with a more refined version of this rustic potato soup. They have developed a highly sophisticated and satisfying soup that consists of a clear stock accompanied by toasted vegetable-cheese croutons. To serve 6, make soup as above and pour through a strainer. Keep the stock hot. Mash vegetables thoroughly and spread them onto 6 slices of freshly toasted and buttered white bread. Top with 5½ oz grated cheese (e.g., Gruyère or Raclette) and toast on the highest rack of a 475°F oven until the cheese melts. Then place bread in soup bowls and pour the soup around the edges. Bon appétit!

Traditional
Invigorating

Greek Rice Soup

SERVES 4:

➤ 1 lemon

3 cloves garlic

4 cups chicken stock

1 bay leaf

$1/3$ cup rice

9 oz small zucchini

2 eggs

2 tsp chopped dill

Salt and pepper

🕐 Prep time: 45 minutes

➤ Calories per serving: 570

1 | Rinse lemon, dry, grate off zest, and squeeze out juice. Peel garlic and cut cloves in half. Bring stock to a boil with lemon zest, garlic, and bay leaf. Add rice and cook for 15 minutes until al dente.

2 | Rinse zucchini, add whole to stock, and simmer soup for another 5 minutes. In the meantime, beat together eggs, lemon juice, dill, and 2 tbs soup until foamy.

3 | Remove cooked zucchini from soup. Remove soup from heat and gradually stir in egg foam. Season soup with salt and pepper and let stand for 2 minutes. In the meantime, slice zucchini and distribute in prewarmed soup bowls. Ladle rice soup over the top and serve.

Exotic | For Company

Caribbean Potato Soup

SERVES 4:

➤ 14 oz white fish filet (e.g., cod)

2 limes

$5^1/2$ oz bacon

2 onions

3 stalks celery

20 cherry tomatoes (9 oz)

14 oz sweet potatoes (may substitute starchy potatoes, such as baking)

5 sprigs fresh thyme

1 small cinnamon stick ($1^1/4$ inch)

$3^1/2$ cups stock

Salt

🕐 Prep time: 50 minutes

🕐 Marinating time: 1 hour

➤ Calories per serving: 870

1 | Cut fish into ¾-inch pieces. Squeeze juice from limes. Mix fish with juice and marinate in the refrigerator for 1 hour.

2 | Cut bacon slices into strips. Peel onions, cut into quarters, and then into strips. Rinse and clean celery, set aside a little of the greens, and slice stalks thinly. Rinse cherry tomatoes, clean, and cut in half. Peel potatoes and slice. Rinse thyme and tie in a bundle with cinnamon stick.

3 | In a wide pot, slowly fry the fat out of the bacon and remove bacon. Sauté onions in the bacon fat until translucent. Pour in stock. Add celery, sweet potatoes, and thyme with cinnamon and simmer gently for 10 minutes. Add tomatoes and simmer for another 5 minutes. Chop celery greens.

4 | Remove soup from heat. Add fish including marinade, celery greens, and bacon, cover, and let stand for 5 minutes. Remove thyme and cinnamon and serve.

Traditional | Served Cold
White Gazpacho

SERVES 4:

➤ 8 slices white sourdough bread or dense white bread (7 oz)

1¼ cup milk

1 clove garlic

3½ oz seedless white grapes

3½ oz ground almonds

⅓ cup extra virgin olive oil

¼ cup sunflower oil

2 tbs sherry vinegar

2 cups mineral water (preferably not very carbonated)

Salt

🕐 Prep time: 35 minutes

🕐 Refrigeration time: 1 hour

➤ Calories per serving: 625

1 | Remove crust from bread, cut into cubes, and soak half in milk. Peel and chop garlic. Rinse grapes, clean, and cut in half.

2 | In a blender or food processor, purée soaked bread including milk, garlic, and almonds, gradually blending in olive and sunflower oil to make a creamy mixture. Stir in vinegar and water. Season Gazpacho with salt, cover, and refrigerate for 1 hour. If necessary, add a little water.

3 | In an ungreased pan, toast remaining bread cubes. Transfer Gazpacho to bowls or glasses and garnish with grapes and bread cubes.

Tex-Mex | Spicy
Tortilla Soup

SERVES 4–6:

➤ 6 flour tortillas (9 oz)

2 cloves garlic

2 white onions

1 red chili pepper

1 bunch cilantro

8 tbs oil

2 tbs tomato paste

6 cups vegetable or chicken stock

Salt

1 avocado

5½ oz grated cheese (e.g. sharp Cheddar)

🕐 Prep time: 50 minutes

➤ Calories per serving (6): 495

1 | Chop half the tortillas coarsely. Peel and dice garlic and onions. Clean chili pepper, remove seeds, and chop. Rinse cilantro, shake dry, and chop leaves.

2 | Braise onions, garlic, chili pepper, and half the cilantro in 2 tbs oil for 3 minutes. Add chopped tortillas and tomato paste and sauté for 1 minute. Pour in stock, season with salt, and simmer gently for 15 minutes. Purée soup and put through a strainer.

3 | Cut avocado in half, remove pit, peel, and dice. Cut remaining tortillas into quarters. For each tortilla, heat 2 tbs oil in a pan and fry 4 tortilla quarters for ½ minute on each side until they become crispy and expand. Heat soup, transfer to bowls, and garnish with diced avocado, grated cheese, and remaining cilantro. Serve with crispy tortillas.

Soups with Style

Now things are going to get a little more sophisticated! These types of soups leave you hungering for more, which is why they make good starters. So pay attention, because you may have to be a little more refined yourself!

Quick Recipes

Carrot Sip

SERVES 4:

➤ 3¹/₂ oz tofu | 1 tsp soy sauce
4 green onions | 3 tbs butter
3 tbs curry powder | 3 cups carrot juice
¹/₃ cup orange juice | Salt | Black pepper

1 | Dice tofu, mix with soy sauce, and
set aside. Rinse green onions, clean, and
remove dark green parts. Cut 1 onion in
half lengthwise and set aside four of the
outer layers. Cut remaining green onions
crosswise into strips and braise in 2 tbs
butter for 5 minutes.

2 | In a second pot, braise curry in
remaining butter for 1 minute. Pour
in juice, bring to a boil, season with salt,
blend until foamy, and pour into tall,
heavy glasses. Add tofu and onion strips,
stick in "onion straws," and grind pepper
over the top.

Chive Soup

SERVES 4:

➤ 4 bunches chives | 3 egg yolks
¹/₂ cup heavy cream
3¹/₂ oz smoked salmon
2¹/₂ cups fish stock
¹/₄ cup white wine
³/₄ cup crème fraîche
Salt | White pepper

1 | Rinse chives and shake dry. Chop 2
bunches coarsely. Cut remaining chives
into fine rings and whisk together with egg
yolks and cream. Cut salmon into strips.

2 | Bring fish stock, wine, and crème
fraîche to a boil and remove from heat.
Stir in coarsely chopped chives and let
stand for 5 minutes. Pour soup through
a strainer. Mix ¹/₂ cup with the egg cream
mixture and stir into the soup. Season
with salt and pepper and reheat without
bringing to a boil. Add salmon.

37

For Special Occasions | Invigorating

Classic Asparagus Cream Soup

SERVES 4:

➤ **9 oz white asparagus**
Salt
1 pinch sugar
3 tbs butter
2 tbs flour
$\frac{1}{2}$ cup dry white wine
3 dashes Worcestershire sauce
1 tbs lemon juice
Cayenne pepper
1 cup heavy cream

⊙ Prep time: 1 hour
➤ Calories per serving: 290

1 | Rinse asparagus, clean, and peel. Cut off tips and, depending on their size, cut lengthwise into halves or quarters and set aside. Bring $3\frac{1}{2}$ cups water to a boil with asparagus peels, 1 tsp salt, and sugar, cover and simmer over low heat for 15 minutes. Pour asparagus peel water through a strainer and into a bowl.

2 | Cut remaining asparagus pieces (excluding tips) into thin slices and braise in 2 tbs butter for 5 minutes. Sprinkle with flour and sauté while stirring until golden. Gradually add wine and asparagus water while stirring and simmer for 10 minutes.

3 | Pour soup through a strainer, squeezing out asparagus pieces thoroughly. Season soup to taste with salt, 1 small pinch cayenne, a few drops Worcestershire sauce, and lemon juice. Beat cream until stiff.

4 | Sauté asparagus tips in 1 tbs butter for 6–8 minutes until al dente and distribute in prewarmed soup bowls. In the meantime, heat asparagus soup and beat with a wire whisk or hand blender. Fold in whipped cream and distribute soup in the bowls. Serve immediately.

TIPS

Wire Whisking

➤ When you add the asparagus water to the roux, make sure the water isn't too hot since this will cause the soup to boil too quickly and lumps might form. Time-saving trick: Let roux cool, then you can add hot water as long as you stir constantly with a wire whisk while adding. Or mix wine and half the water, add it while stirring, and then add the rest. And always simmer it for 10 minutes so it won't taste floury.

➤ Whisking the soup and whipped cream will make the soup nice and foamy. Even better: Finish the soup by adding a small shot of champagne to produce superior foam.

➤ You can make this soup a little richer by adding strips of cooked ham or marinated salmon, a few croutons, and a little chervil or tarragon.

Vegetarian

Green Fennel Soup

SERVES 4:

➤ 3 cups puréed
  frozen spinach (9 oz)
  2 small fennel bulbs (28 oz)
  1 onion
  2 cloves garlic
  2 tbs raisins
  1 tbs dried oregano
  6 tbs olive oil
  5 cups vegetable stock
  Salt and pepper
  2 oz whole Parmesan

🕐 Prep time: 1 hour
🕐 Thawing time: 1 hour
➤ Calories per serving: 320

1 | Thaw spinach. Rinse fennel, clean, and cut into quarters. Cut out core and dice quarters. Peel onion and garlic and dice. Rinse raisins.

2 | Braise fennel, onion, garlic, and oregano in 2 tbs olive oil for 5 minutes. Pour in vegetable stock and simmer fennel for 15–20 minutes until tender.

3 | Add spinach and simmer for another 5 minutes. Season soup with salt and pepper. Let cool slightly and purée in a blender, in a food processor, or with a hand blender.

4 | Add raisins. Bring soup to a boil and then transfer to bowls. Drizzle in remaining olive oil and shave Parmesan over the top.

Traditional with a Twist
Inexpensive

Root Vegetable Soup

SERVES 4.

➤ 1 leek
  3 parsnips
  3 carrots
  3 1/2 oz potatoes
  3 tbs butter
  4 cups vegetable stock
  Salt
  Pepper
  Nutmeg
  1 bunch parsley
  2 cups buttermilk

🕐 Prep time: 1 1/4 hours
➤ Calories per serving: 200

1 | Clean leek, remove dark green part, cut in half lengthwise, rinse well, and cut into wide strips. Peel and dice parsnips, carrots, and potatoes.

2 | Braise leek in 2 tbs butter for 5 minutes. Add and braise parsnips and carrots for 1 minute, then add potatoes and vegetable stock. Season soup with salt, pepper, and nutmeg and simmer for 30 minutes until the vegetables are tender. In the meantime, rinse parsley, shake dry, and chop leaves.

3 | Mash finished soup with a potato masher, put through a sieve, add buttermilk, and heat. Season to taste with salt and pepper. Heat remaining butter with parsley until it foams up and stir into the soup.

Mediterranean | Easy
Roasted Tomato Soup

SERVES 4:

➤ 3¹/₃ lbs ripe
   plum tomatoes
   4 cloves garlic
   1 bunch basil
   7 tbs olive oil
   2 small slices Italian bread
   1³/₄ cups vegetable stock
   Salt
   Pepper
   1 pinch sugar
   2 oz whole Parmesan

🕐 Prep time: 25 minutes
🕐 Cooking time: 1 hour
➤ Calories per serving: 310

1 | Rinse tomatoes, remove cores, and cut in half. Peel garlic and cut into quarters. Rinse basil, shake dry, chop leaves, and set aside stems.

2 | Preheat oven to 350°F. In a wide baking dish, mix together tomatoes, 5 tbs oil, and garlic. Add basil stems and bake in the oven (middle rack) for 1 hour. Then remove basil stems and discard.

3 | Dice bread. In a pot, bring to a boil bread, tomatoes (including cooking liquid), and vegetable stock. Purée, put through a coarse sieve, and heat. Stir in chopped basil and season to taste with salt, pepper, and sugar. Drizzle with remaining oil and shave Parmesan over the top.

Traditional
Heartwarming
Cream of Tomato Soup

SERVES 4:

➤ 2 oz bacon
   1 onion
   1 small carrot
   1 juniper berry
   1 tbs flour
   2 cups meat or
   vegetable stock
   1 large (28-oz) can
   peeled tomatoes
   Salt
   Pepper
   Sugar
   1 bunch chives
   ¹/₂ cup heavy cream

🕐 Prep time: 40 minutes
➤ Calories per serving: 240

1 | Dice bacon. Peel onion and carrot and dice. Crush juniper berry with a heavy pot.

2 | In a large pot, fry the fat out of the bacon over medium heat and remove from pot. Braise onion, carrot, and juniper berry in the bacon fat for 5 minutes, then add and brown flour. Pour in stock while stirring. Stir in tomatoes including juice and season with salt, pepper, and sugar. Simmer soup for 15 minutes, purée, and put through a sieve.

3 | Rinse chives, shake dry, and cut into rings. Beat cream until stiff. Heat tomato soup and stir in chives and bacon. Serve soup in cups or bowls topped with a dollop of whipped cream.

Exotic | Vegetarian
Ginger-Pumpkin Soup

SERVES 4:

- 1 piece pumpkin (1 lb)
  1 small onion
  1 small starchy potato
  2 pieces ginger (each the size of a walnut)
  1 (14-oz) can unsweetened coconut milk
  2 tsp red curry paste (may substitute 2 tbs curry powder)
  1¾ cup vegetable stock
  Salt
  2 tbs pumpkin seeds
  ¼ cup oil

⏱ Prep time: 50 minutes
- Calories per serving: 180

1 | Remove seeds from pumpkin, peel, and dice. Peel onion and dice finely. Peel potato and dice to size of pumpkin pieces. Peel ginger and slice each piece lengthwise. Leave half of these slices whole and cut the other half into thin strips.

2 | Carefully open can of coconut milk. Take 1 tbs of the thick cream off the top and set aside. Heat remaining cream in a large pot, setting aside coconut milk. Stir in onions, ginger strips, and curry paste and braise gently for 5 minutes. Add diced pumpkin and braise for another 1–2 minutes.

3 | Add remaining coconut milk from the can, vegetable stock, and potato and salt lightly. Simmer for 20 minutes until vegetables are tender, then mash with a potato masher or purée and, if desired, put through a sieve.

4 | In an ungreased pan, toast pumpkin seeds. In a small pot, heat oil and sauté remaining ginger slices for 1–2 minutes until crispy. Heat pumpkin soup, transfer to soup bowls, and garnish with coconut cream, pumpkin seeds, and fried ginger slices.

TIPS

About the Ingredients

- Pumpkin has an intense, slightly acidic flavor, but you can also use other types of squash such as kabocha or butternut. These two are especially aromatic.

- You'll find coconut milk and curry paste in an Asian market or in the exotic foods section of a well-stocked supermarket. Make sure the coconut milk is unsweetened and contains no preservatives (read the list of ingredients).

- To make the ginger slices especially crispy, heat at least 2 cups oil to 350°F, deep-fry ginger slices for 1 minute, and then drain on paper towels.

Heartwarming
Inexpensive

Eggplant Soup with Feta

SERUES 4:

- ➤ 2¹/₄ lbs eggplant
- 2 cloves garlic
- 1 white onion
- 1 large bunch parsley
- 4 anchovies
- 7 oz feta cubes in oil (from a jar)
- 3 cups chicken stock
- Salt | Pepper

🕓 Prep time: 1¹/₄ hours

➤ Calories per serving: 540

1 | Preheat oven to 350°F. Rinse eggplants and bake in the oven along with unpeeled garlic cloves for 30–40 minutes until tender. Let cool slightly.

2 | In the meantime, peel onion and dice finely. Rinse parsley, shake dry, and chop leaves coarsely. Rinse anchovies briefly and chop. Cut cooked eggplants in half lengthwise and scrape out interior with a spoon. Squeeze garlic out of the peel.

3 | In a pot, gently heat 2 tbs oil from the jar of feta and braise onions and anchovies for 5 minutes. Add eggplant and garlic and braise briefly. Pour in stock, season with salt and pepper, and simmer for 15 minutes.

4 | Drain feta and mix with parsley. Purée cooked soup with half the feta mixture and reheat. Distribute soup in bowls and sprinkle with remaining feta cubes.

Sophisticated
Can Prepare in Advance

Celery Soup

SERVES 4:

- ➤ 1 celery root with greens
- 1 onion
- 5¹/₂ oz Gorgonzola
- 3 tbs butter
- 5 cups chicken stock
- Salt | pepper
- 5 slices sandwich bread (3¹/₂ oz)
- 1 cup heavy cream

🕓 Prep time: 1 hour

➤ Calories per serving: 715

1 | Pluck off a handful of tender leaves from the celery root and rinse thoroughly. Clean celery root, rinse, peel, and dice. Peel onion and dice finely. Dice cheese.

2 | Braise onion in butter over low heat for 5 minutes. Add celery root and braise for another 5 minutes. Pour in chicken stock and season with salt and pepper. Simmer for 15–20 minutes until celery root is al dente.

3 | Remove crusts from bread, dice, add, and simmer with the celery root for another 5 minutes until the celery root is tender. Remove one-fourth of the soup and bring to a boil with the celery greens. Add cream to the rest of the soup, heat, and melt 3¹/₂ oz Gorgonzola in it. Purée both soups.

4 | Heat both soups. Distribute white celery soup in wide bowls and ladle the green over the top. Decorate soup artistically with a fork and sprinkle with remaining Gorgonzola.

Traditional with a New Twist | Can Prepare in Advance

Corn Chowder

SERVES 4:

- 4 fresh ears of corn
  1 onion
  4 thin slices of bacon
  2 tbs butter
  Salt
  1 bay leaf
  1 bunch chives
  ¼ cup heavy cream
  5½ oz cooked and peeled shrimp
  1 tbs hot mustard

⏲ Prep time: 1¼ hours

➤ Calories per serving: 540

1 | Clean corn (see below) and rinse. Cut kernels from ears. Peel onion and dice finely.

2 | In a large pot, fry bacon in the butter over low heat until crispy. Remove and let cool. Braise onions in this fat for 5 minutes, then add corn kernels and braise for another 5 minutes. Add 4 cups water, season with salt, add bay leaf, and simmer for 30–40 minutes until the corn is tender.

3 | Rinse chives, shake dry, and cut into rings. Remove bay leaf, purée soup, and put through a sieve. Cut bacon into pieces.

4 | Stir cream into soup and bring to a boil. Stir in chives, shrimp, and mustard, cover, remove from heat, and let stand for 2 minutes. Transfer to soup bowls and garnish with bacon pieces.

1 Shuck corn
Pull back leaves and pull off silk.

2 Remove leaves
Then break off stem with leaves.

3 Remove kernels
With a knife, cut off kernels down the length of the ear.

49

Clear Cups

Since good things really do take time, we'll finish this book with soups in their most pure, unadulterated forms—broths and consommés simply brimming with flavor.

Quick Recipes

Essence of Garlic Broth

SERVES 4:

➤ 10 cloves garlic | 2 sage leaves
1 whole clove | 5 white peppercorns
Salt | 3 tbs olive oil | 4 slices baguette
4 tbs grated cheese

1 | Peel garlic and rinse sage leaves. Bring
4 cups water to a boil with garlic, sage,
spices, 1 tsp salt, and 1 tbs oil, simmer
gently for 10–12 minutes, and then set
aside for 5 minutes.

2 | In the meantime, toast baguette slices
on both sides either under the broiler or
in a pan. Sprinkle with cheese and place
under broiler until cheese melts slightly.
Pour soup through a strainer, heat, and
transfer to wide bowls. Set croutons on
top and drizzle with remaining oil.

Miso Soup

SERVES 4:

➤ 7 oz tofu (not too firm) | 1 green onion
4 cups dashi (Japanese stock made
from dried fish and seaweed; use
instant available from Asian market)
2½ oz light miso (soy bean paste
from Asian market)

1 | Cut tofu into ½-inch cubes. Rinse
green onion, clean, and cut into very
thin rings.

2 | Prepare dashi according to package
directions, bring to a boil, and remove
from heat. Holding a sieve in the hot
liquid, press miso through the sieve with
a wooden spoon and stir into soup. Bring
soup just to the point of boiling, remove
from stove, add tofu and green onion,
and let stand for 5 minutes. Ladle soup
into bowls and sip slowly.

51

Asian | Heartwarming
Spicy Shrimp Soup

SERVES 4:

➤ **8 large unpeeled shrimp, fresh or frozen**

2 stalks lemon grass

1 piece fresh ginger (walnut-sized)

2 red chili peppers

1 bunch cilantro

5 tbs Asian fish sauce (may substitute soy sauce)

4 cups chicken stock

3 tbs cornstarch

3 tbs rice or sherry vinegar

🕐 Prep time: 40 minutes

🕐 Cooling time: $1^1/_2$ hours

➤ Calories per serving: 590

1 | Thaw frozen shrimp. Peel shrimp, cut a slit down the back, and remove veins with a pointy knife. Rinse and cut in half lengthwise. Also rinse shells.

2 | Rinse lemon grass and pound flat with a pot or meat cleaver. Peel ginger and cut into thin slices. Rinse chili peppers, cut in half lengthwise, and remove seeds. Rinse cilantro, shake dry, pull off leaves, and set aside stems.

3 | Bring stock to a boil with shrimp shells, lemon grass, ginger, chili peppers, cilantro stems, and fish sauce and simmer gently for 15 minutes. Remove from heat, let cool completely, and pour through a strainer.

4 | Heat soup, then add shrimp and simmer until pink and cooked throughout. Whisk together cornstarch and vinegar, stir into hot soup, and bring to a boil. Add cilantro and serve in bowls. For a heartier soup, you can add in cooked rice vermicelli noodles.

TIPS

Traditional, Spicy Soup

➤ This is a moderate version of a traditional Asian soup. If you want the spicy original, double the number of chili peppers and don't remove the seeds. In this case you'll need 2–3 tsp sugar for balance and a lot of staying power!

➤ To make a heartier (but also cloudier) soup, at the very end stir 2 whisked egg yolks into the gently simmering liquid.

Traditional
Can Prepare in Advance

Consommé with Chives

SERVES 8:

- 1 1/3 lbs beef bones (not marrow bones)
- 1 each carrot, celery root, and parsnip
- 1 leek
- 1/2 onion
- 1 3/4 lbs beef stew meat
- 1 chicken thigh
- 5 peppercorns
- 1 bunch chives
- Salt

⏲ Prep time: 30 minutes
⏲ Cooking time: 4 hours
➤ Calories per serving: 75

1 | Boil beef bones in water for 1 minute, then rinse under cold water. Place in a pot with 12 cups water and slowly bring to a boil. Simmer gently for 2 hours, occasionally skimming off foam.

2 | Peel carrot, celery root, and parsnip. Remove dark green part from leek, cut in half lengthwise, and rinse well. Rinse onion with the skin on and roast in an ungreased pan with the cut side down until dark. Add stew meat, chicken thigh, onion, peppercorns, carrot, celery root, parsnip, and leek to the bones and simmer for 1 1/2 to 2 hours until meat and vegetables are tender.

3 | Remove meat, bones, and vegetables from the soup. Ladle into a strainer lined with cheesecloth and remove fat. Rinse chives, shake dry, and cut into rings. Season soup with salt, bring to a boil, and serve in cups with the chives.

Mediterranean
For Special Occasions

Cherry Tomato Tea

SERVES 4:

- 2 3/4 lbs cherry tomatoes
- 2 shallots
- 1 bunch tarragon
- 1/4 tsp black peppercorns
- Salt
- 2 tbs medium dry sherry (may substitute water)
- 1 tsp sugar
- 3 1/2 oz white fish filet

⏲ Prep time: 35 minutes
⏲ Marinating time: 4 hours
⏲ Refrigeration time: 12 hours
➤ Calories per serving: 40

1 | Rinse tomatoes and set aside 3 1/2 oz. Cut remaining tomatoes in half and dice larger ones. Peel shallots and dice. Rinse tarragon and shake dry. Set aside 1 sprig and pull leaves off the rest. Crush peppercorns.

2 | Boil 2 cups water with 1 tbs salt, add the shallots, and cook for 5 minutes, then add tomato halves, tarragon leaves, peppercorns, sherry, and sugar and marinate at room temperature for 4 hours.

3 | Suspend a large strainer in a deep bowl and pour in tomatoes. Weight down with a plate and a small pot full of water on top and let drain in the refrigerator for 12 hours.

4 | Clean remaining tomatoes and cut into wedges. Cut fish into thin slices. Pull off remaining tarragon leaves. Heat tomato tea. Place tomatoes, fish, and tarragon in prewarmed cups and pour tomato tea over the top. Serve immediately.

◄ Photo top: **Consommé with Chives**   Photo bottom: **Cherry Tomato Tea**

Asian | Vegetarian

Corn Soup

SERVES 4:

- ➤ 3 fresh ears of corn
  4 green onions
  1 piece ginger
  (walnut-sized)
  1 tbs oil
  5 cups vegetable stock
  2 tbs Chinese rice wine
  (may substitute mild
  sherry or water)
  1 tsp sugar
  4 tbs soy sauce
  1–2 tsp sesame oil
  (may substitute toasted
  sesame seeds)

⏱ Prep time: 45 minutes
➤ Calories per serving: 330

1 | Shuck corn, remove silk, and rinse. Cut kernels from cobs (see page 49). Rinse and clean green onions, removing dark green parts. Cut into thin slices and set aside 4 tbs. Peel ginger and grate finely.

2 | Stir-fry green onions and ginger in the oil over high heat for 1 minute. Add corn and sauté briefly.

3 | Pour in stock and bring to a boil. Add rice wine, sugar, and soy sauce and simmer for 20–30 minutes until corn is al dente. Transfer corn soup to bowls, sprinkle with remaining green onions, and drizzle with sesame oil.

Inexpensive
For Company

French Onion Soup

SERVES 4:

- ➤ For the soup:
  $1^{1}/_{2}$ lbs onions
  3 tbs butter
  1 tsp sugar
  1 pinch cayenne pepper
  1 cup dry white wine (may substitute beef stock)
  1 lbs flour
  5 cups beef stock
  Salt
- ➤ For the croutons:
  Sliced baguette (9 oz)
  3 oz grated Gruyère
  $1^{1}/_{2}$ oz freshly grated Parmesan
  1–2 tsp Dijon mustard

⏱ Prep time: $1^{1}/_{4}$ hours
➤ Calories per serving: 500

1 | Peel onions and cut into thin rings. In a wide pot, melt butter. Add onions, cover, and braise over medium heat for 10 minutes. Sprinkle with sugar and cayenne and braise, uncovered, over low heat for 20 minutes while stirring until the onions are golden brown.

2 | Pour in $^{1}/_{2}$ cup wine and reduce. Add and brown flour for 2 minutes. Add stock and remaining wine and simmer gently for 30 minutes.

3 | For the croutons, toast baguette slices on both sides either under the broiler or in a toaster. Combine Gruyère, Parmesan, and mustard and spread on bread. Broil bread until the cheese melts. Transfer hot soup to bowls, set croutons on top, and serve.

TIP | French Onion Soup is traditionally prepared with beef stock but if you'd prefer to avoid it, you can also substitute vegetable stock.

Asian | Sophisticated

Salmon au jus

➤ SERVES 4:

1 piece ginger (walnut-sized)

3 green onions

4 cups chicken stock

3 tbs Asian fish sauce (may substitute soy sauce)

1/2 cup Chinese rice wine (may substitute mild sherry or stock)

1 tbs sugar

1 star anise (may substitute 1/4 tsp anise seed)

1 cucumber

4 (3 1/2-oz) salmon filets

Salt

1 tbs oil

2 tbs sweet chili sauce

🕙 Prep time: 30 minutes

🕙 Cooking time: 1 hour

➤ Calories per serving: 820

1 | Peel ginger and cut into thin slices. Rinse green onions, clean, and cut up. Combine these two ingredients with stock, fish sauce, rice wine, sugar, and anise and simmer gently over low heat for 1 hour, then pour through a fine strainer.

2 | In the meantime, peel cucumber, cut in half lengthwise, and scrape out seeds with a spoon. Cut cucumber halves on an angle into long, thin slices.

3 | Season stock to taste and heat. Salt salmon and fry in a pan in hot oil for 2 minutes on each side, then keep warm under tented foil. In the same pan, braise cucumbers, 5 tbs seasoned stock, and chili sauce for 2–3 minutes, then season with salt. Heap cucumber in prewarmed soup bowls and pour on just enough stock to cover the cucumber. Set the salmon on top and serve.

TIPS

Asian Stew

➤ Salmon au jus is a modern Asian version of stew. The intensely flavored stock is intended to be a sauce that accompanies the fish rather than a soup to fill your bowl —in other words, the salmon shouldn't be swimming.

➤ You'll find these typical ingredients in an Asian market or the ethnic foods section of a well-stocked supermarket. If you can't find fish sauce, substitute soy sauce. Chinese rice wine can easily be replaced with a mild sherry. If you use the Japanese rice wine mirin, reduce the amount of sugar because it is very sweet.

ABBREVIATIONS
lb = pound
oz = ounce
tsp = teaspoon
tbs = tablespoon

The Author

Sebastian Dickhaut ives in Munich where he is both a journalist and an author of books. After spending seven gastronomical years mastering a wide range of soup styles from the traditional to the contemporary, he turned his talents to writing about food. At the same time, his repertoire of soups was supplemented both by his experience cooking for his young family and through living in Vienna and Sydney. When he returned to Germany, he put together this collection of his favorites. He is co-creator of the bestselling "Basic Cooking" series and also wrote the GU Kitchen Guides on casseroles and potatoes.

The Photographer

Kai Mewes is an independent food photographer in Munich who works for publishers and in advertising. His studio and test kitchen are located near Munich's famous Viktualienmarkt. His appetizing photos reflect his dedication to combining photography and culinary pleasure. Food styling in this book is the work of Akos Neuberger

Photo Credits

FoodPhotographie Eising, Martina Görlach: cover photo
Stockfood: pages 4 (top), 10 (top)
All others: Kai Mewes, Munich

Published originally under the title Suppen; von Klassik bis Kult © 2002 Gräfe und Unzer Verlag GmbH, Munich. English translation for the North America market © 2002, Silverback Books, Inc.

Editors: Elizabeth Penn, Stefanie Poziombka
Translator: Christie Tam
Reader: Susanne Bodensteiner
Layout, typography and cover design: Independent Medien Design, Munich
Production: Patty Holden and Maike Harmeier

Printed in China

ISBN 1-930603-95-9

Enjoy Other Quick & Easy Books

Marlisa Szwillus

Fondue

Cheese, vegetable, or all kinds of meat—enjoy them all right at the table. More than 50 recipes

Cornelia Adam

Salads

An array of salads to eat as appetizers, entrées, and party dishes. Includes classic choices and cutting-edge alternatives.

Sebastian Dickhaut

Sandwiches

Nutritious, open-faced healthy sandwiches and fillings

Xenia Burgtorf

Cornelia Adam

Quiche

Delicious, savory pies with vegetables, meat, poultry, or fish—serve for all occasions

Cornelia Adam

Garlic

Sophisticated Recipes with the Favorite Spice of the Mediterranean Region. Spicy (tangy), Fine (delicate), international

Cornelia Schinharl

Easy Vegetarian

Uncomplicated and sophisticated — Vegetarian recipes for all seasons

Sebastian Dickhaut

Casseroles

Anette Heisch

Oil & Vinegar

A wonderful source of information, delicious recipes, and helpful hints—liven up your favorite dishes and

Andreas Fürtmayr

Sushi

Classic ideas from Japan—Home-made perfectly

1 Noodle, 50 Sauces

Everyday Pasta • Old and New Italian Dishes • Noodle biography • 50 Tips for Success

Healthy Wok

Einstein Dorn
Christian Willrich
Jochz Rebov

Great freshness and satisfying meals

Antje Gruener

Grilling

Gina Greifenstein

1 Batter— 50 Cakes

Baking to your heart's content

Cooking in Clay

Healthy Recipes with Great Flavor

Erika Casparek-Türkkan

Doris Muliar

Cocktails for Drivers

100% Enjoyment

Antipasti and Tapas

Mediterranean Appetizers
Cornelia Schinharl

Soups

Classic to Contemporary

Sebastian Dickhaut

Claudia Schmidt

Raclette

New Recipes with Cheese Primer and Party Dips

THE RIGHT TOOLS

- A soup chef needs two pots—one that holds about 5 quarts for stocks and one that holds about 3 quarts for the soup itself. Better yet is a third 1-quart pot for soup garnishes, etc.
- Standard equipment for the finishing touches includes a fine sieve for straining (even better: a cheesecloth for straining clear soups), ladle, potato masher, wire whisk, and hand blender.

Guaranteed Success with Soups

FLAVOR THROUGH BRAISING

- Many soups take on more flavor if you briefly braise the vegetables beforehand.
- Start with onions (may also include herbs or seasonings) in oil or butter to set the basic tone, then add vegetables at staggered intervals according to cooking times.
- Exceptions: Starchy vegetables like potatoes and watery vegetables like tomatoes.

FRESH HERBS

- Firmer herbs such as marjoram, oregano, rosemary, sage, and thyme, whether fresh or dried, need 10–15 minutes for their flavor to unfold fully.
- Tender herbs such as basil, dill, parsley, and chives should be dried off, chopped coarsely, and stirred into the hot soup at the very end.

FINDING A BALANCE

- True soup artists taste the contents of the pot every now and then to get a feel for the right blend of flavors.
- With this knowledge, you can begin to predict the final flavor early on and then direct it accordingly.